TEMPERA PAINTING

TEMPERA PAINTING

By

ZOLTAN SEPESHY

AMERICAN STUDIO BOOKS
NEW YORK AND LONDON

ACKNOWLEDGMENTS

We wish to thank the Midtown Galleries, New York, for their generous help in supplying photographs of the author's work for reproduction in this volume. Acknowledgments are due also to the Museums and collectors who have kindly given permission for paintings in their possession to be reproduced. Mr. Sepeshy would also like to thank the contributing artists for permission to include examples of their tempera paintings at the end of the volume for purposes of the student's analysis and comparison.

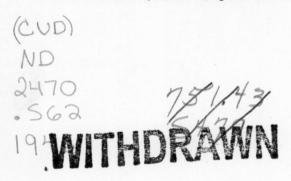
Copyright 1946, Holme Press, Incorporated
New York

Printed in U.S.A. by Handford Brown Co.
Coytesville, N. J.

Foreword

To know how to paint is not the same thing as to paint well, but in order to paint well it is necessary to know how to paint. Although sound techniques, like good manners, ought not to be singled out for approbation, their absence may be deplored. They are a means through which a personality is expressed, an idea given shape, an inspiration put into form.

Technique thus becomes the vehicle of the idea and gives wings to inspiration. Expertness of execution should be adequate for effective communication; the degree of effectiveness may be measured by the quality of abandon with which an artist can express himself.

It is the freedom of spontaneity which is the ultimate goal of the accomplished artist. Without a mastery of skill and techniques he fails to reveal his intention; on the other hand, he must curb his performance in skill if he sees that his interest in techniques is overwhelming the idea he attempts to portray.

A happy result has been obtained by the artist when the observer looks upon his work and sees the idea, standing forth in full power, adequately but inconspicuously supported by the technique.

And so it is that every craftsman who wants to say something worthwhile and permanent must become an artist, and every artist who has something significant and valuable to say must become a craftsman.

You bought this book, no doubt, because you wished to improve your craftsmanship. Certain skills and techniques are described here in detail for you. If you follow them carefully you may become a craftsman who is taking determined steps on the road to becoming an artist, or you may be an artist who is learning to master the crafts he needs in order to speak clearly and coherently in the world of art.

Goethe once said, "Only a part of art can be taught." This book contains a discussion of that part of art which can be taught. Zoltan Sepeshy is a good teacher; he has designed these discussions to help you learn to paint with skill and permanence. The rest is up to you.

ALBERT CHRIST-JANER

Cranbrook Academy of Art
1946

Introduction

Since the approach to tempera here presented is technical rather than historical, consideration of the early uses of this medium is somewhat superfluous. Furthermore, many contemporary works on traditional tempera techniques are readily available. Here we are concerned with technical values offered by tempera with which the reader may be less familiar.

It is of passing interest to note that the use of tempera was probably started very early in the development of art. The Egyptians might have used an egg binder for the pigments on sarcophagi. Pliny refers to two media employed by Greek painters, one of which may have been egg tempera.

Scholars of European art have found that tempera had fairly wide use by the 13th Century. It is doubtful whether it was used in the Western World before the 13th Century. Cenini, in the 15th Century, discussed tempera at length in his work on the techniques of painting, while Vasari, in the 16th Century, mentions an egg medium in his book, *Lives of Painters*.

Since both artists and eggs antedate historical records, there is no reason to doubt that albuminous and colloidal vehicles were discovered early in the history of painting. What is of greater importance is the fact that the use of tempera tended to decline in modern art, since oil was found to be a more fluent binder for pigments.

The claim tempera has for extensive contemporary revival is that it possesses possibilities not before fully realized and certainly not widely exploited. It cannot justify itself as a mere competitor of oil. This book points to objectives tempera can attain in its own right, values unique to this medium. Not as a rival medium, seeking the same ends as other media, but rather as another and equally important medium must tempera find its future place in art.

Z. S.

7

Tempera—Why

To paint or not to paint?

That is no longer the question if you are exploring the recently developed possibilities of tempera as a medium. For the chances are that you are already painting with other media—pastel, water color, gouache, oil— and that you are in quest of a luminous, a rich medium into which you may translate some already accomplished, and perhaps favorite, work.

If you are considering tempera as a medium, you must rid your mind of misconceptions. You must not think of tempera in its earlier historical use. Indeed, you must not even think of its most usual recent use. You must be prepared to take a new road, to break with past habit, to prove that at least in painting there is something new under the sun.

William James called pragmatism "a new name for some old ways of thinking." Tempera, in its recently developed modes, is an old name for a new way of painting. Perhaps that is why you are turning to it—not as to a somewhat outworn medium, but rather as to a vehicle of certain values to be found in no other medium.

Would you cut a beefsteak with a toothbrush?

If you tried, would you then throw the toothbrush away as a useless instrument? Would it not be wiser to examine its possibilities and see whether a more valid use for a toothbrush might not be found?

To use tempera as an opaque medium to give opacity to the pigments by mixing them with white—indeed, mixing them on the palette with each other—is to ignore the most distinctive qualities I have found in tempera and to force it into a function more easily accomplished by oil or gouache or a mixed technique.

Many great artists have used opaque tempera to paint many beautiful pictures. Three superb examples are reproduced on the succeeding pages. Yet a critic may well ask, "But why, in heaven's name, does an artist go to the trouble of working with this stubborn medium when the same results could have been achieved with, say, a much more fluent oil paint?"

Tempera might have been consigned to Limbo, its use might have become outmoded, had its new qualities not been brought to light. Its excellent pigments might have found their only use in that allied but very different medium, gouache. It is time now to consider the long neglected values of tempera in comparison with the better known values that other media possess.

GIOVANNI BELLINI   SAINT PETER

MADONNA AND CHILD

PESSELINO

This is an example of perfection in composition and a superb use of tempera in its earlier technical application. Note the subtle modeling in which the brush strokes follow form.

CARLO CRIVELLI   PIETÀ (Detail)

A beautiful early use of egg tempera with white. Note the linear and cross-hatched application of the pigments.

Water color is a fresh and luminous medium. Its transparency gives it both delicacy and clarity. In contrast with many other media, however, it lacks "body"—one layer of water color cannot be applied over another without merging into it physically as well as visually. Would it not be a work of beauty if one color layer could be put on another and the transparency of the paint allow you to see through all these colors at once? Instead, each brush stroke washes out and takes into its own being the brush stroke that underlies it.

Oil paint, and also gouache, have the body that water color lacks. But they haven't the transparency of water color. Their opacity is at once a virtue and a detriment. Each brush stroke hides what underlies it. Hence, oil, for example, may be used quickly and with large strokes. Mistakes are easily covered and corrected, and changes of artistic objective are easily accomplished.

That fragile medium, pastel, is better adapted than any other traditional medium to a peculiar kind of "mixing"—a two-dimensional blending that enhances its color range. Not that this is the only technique adapted to this medium, but fine chalk lines and cross-hatchings may be used to bring different colors close together for the eye to combine. For example, fine parallel and crossed lines of red and blue will be visually perceived as the special kind of purple that the painter is seeking to create.

All these media have their own unique being, nor would I forswear them in favor of tempera. I hope that I shall always continue undogmatically to seek my artistic goals by any means that are adapted to my inclination, to the values I am looking for, to the time at my disposal.

In tempera, however, I have found the possibility of combining the qualities of these other media. It may be used with the transparence and translucence of water color. It may be used with a fine cross-hatching of lines so that the eye mixes and blends the colors two-dimensionally on the surface. It has the "body" for application in layers; yet, when applied in a certain way as pure colors, no layer hides the layers underneath.

As you will see, it is this last property that gives tempera, as I here describe it, more than a mere combination of other qualities, that gives it unique being in its own right. It was through experiments with tempera pigment in gouache that this new and exciting value first became apparent to me. This was the new road that opened before me, a road which I invite other painters, both veterans and beginners, to explore.

How shall I explain this value possessed by tempera by virtue of the fact that it is at once translucent and can be applied in layers without marring that translucence? If you hold up a transparent piece of blue glass and then cover it with a piece of red glass, you will see these colors combine into purple just as if they were mixed on a palette. By using only pure tempera colors unmixed with white and by applying them thinly and finely, I have been able to overlay colors and to achieve just this kind of vertical blending.

"So what?" the reader at this point may well ask. "Why go to all that trouble? Why isn't the result just what you'd get if you mixed your paints right on the palette?"

The answer lies in the fact that the only white in my temperas is *behind* all the other layers of colors, on the board itself. The light by which we see the painting—in fact, the light in the painting itself—is reflected from the very basic background. It is like the light given by nature: it is all-pervasive; it is obscured by that shadow, blotted out by that wall, filtered by this tree; yet back of all things and through all things light is there.

Look at an oil painting. Here a cloud covers the sun. The light from the sun that is behind the cloud must be pictured by the use of *superimposed* degrees of white. The cloud in a tempera painting can let the light through its rifts and tenuous edges from a sun that is *really* behind, from the light that is the background itself, the light that is most vivid before the painting is even begun.

The foregoing comparison of media is not invidiously made. It would be absurd to label tempera "best" among media. There is no *best* medium. Each has its place, its function, its proper use. Each relates fundamentally to individual taste and artistic ends-in-view.

Let us put last things first in this chapter. Let us see what values a tempera may express before we learn precisely with what tools and technique these values may be attained. Let us, in effect, analyze the gross anatomy of a tempera painting before turning our attention to the processes involved.

I have already explained some of the qualities of tempera which lead me each year to transpose a few pictures into this medium. The important point to remember is that my use of tempera is a departure from tradition because I seek objectives that traditional methods hardly give. True, I use the same emulsion that is used in other kinds of tempera painting; therefore my medium must be labeled "tempera." But one important modification is that I use no white pigment; the white, and therefore the light, which comes through—is reflected—from the board or canvas itself. Another modification of major importance is that the medium may be applied with hardly any appreciable pigment depth, or thickness. The third modification is one of technique: by virtue of fine cross-hatching and resultant blending of color lines, I am able to achieve a horizontal color blending as well as a vertical color blending, such as I have described in the preceding pages.

Now, this last paragraph is of great importance in relation to the use of tempera that I am discussing. It is the rationale of tempera itself, its *raison d'être*, the exploitation of the qualities that are uniquely its own. In a sense, all the technical processes set forth in the next chapter pertain to these modifications in the use of tempera.

I may begin a tempera painting by perceiving certain qualities in one of my already completed water colors or gouaches—or, less frequently, oils. I "fall in love" with its tempera possibilities. Or I may turn to sketches and drawings and notes that I made some time ago with an eventual tempera painting in mind. I decide that my projected tempera work deserves my next few weeks, and that I am ready for one of the confining, but exciting, sessions of tempera painting that capture me each year.

Since I am a methodical sort of fellow, my board is already prepared—how, you will learn in the next chapter. All that I need say here is that the board is white, but a very carefully prepared white, for it will never be completely hidden; it will be the source of light for the entire painting, the only white pigment employed.

The final stage preparatory to the painting is a precise line drawing in the exact size of the painting which I transfer to the board in such a manner that it will not "bloom" through even a thin film of paint. The "how" of this will also be explained later.

Now here, with the painting itself, is where experience and long experimentation must bear fruit. No color that I apply is in itself the color of my preliminary sketches. There is a thin, transparent underpainting that carries dominant tones (not necessarily colors) and designs and patterns of the ultimate painting. Then there are several layers, translucent, each of which blends with the pigment that underlies it. I use only pure colors: unmixed, as I have already said, with white. The blending of colors, their modification into varied shades and tones, must depend upon *horizontal* juxtaposition of fine lines and vertical superposition of the fifteen to twenty-five colors that I use.

Note here, for it is very important, the technical possibilities this unique medium gives me for the values I seek. I can run the gamut from transparency to opacity, and I can blend colors in all directions, not on the palette, but on the board itself. I can let white—and light—through from the background or blot it out at will, and I can tone it to any degree. It is diffused, and infuses the painting, just as nature would have it.

Let us see just how the degrees from transparency to opacity are achieved. Thinly applied, tempera is transparent for color—hence the possibility of blending the successive layers of color. For transparency of pattern, where it is desired, one need only space his lines of color sufficiently apart to show what he wants from the preceding layer. Through the thin layers comes the light, reflected from the white background. It is this translucence that makes for the clarity, the luminosity, and the color blending that is so fascinating in tempera painting.

Where a considerable degree of opacity is needed, very close cross-hatching of lines or even solid brush strokes will achieve the result.

Color intensity and dominance, in the "vertical" blending of colors, depend upon the closeness or density of the cross-hatched lines. The more densely they are painted, the more of that color there will be in the specified area. For example, if I want to paint a green that is dominantly yellow, my underpainting may be yellow, or I may have a *dense* network of yellow lines, and on top of them I may have more widely spaced lines of blue and green.

Let me summarize briefly. Beginning with a background of white, I apply successive layers of colors in a manner ranging from wide cross-hatching to close cross-hatching, and, occasionally, solid strokes. The consequence is a horizontal and vertical blend of color that in a medium like oil can be achieved mainly beforehand on the palette, and then with important qualitative differences. The qualities attained in tempera are the translucence of the painting, the diffusion of light.

The objective must always be in sight in this tempera technique, and with each layer of color that the painter applies, he must know its function in relation to all subsequent layers. Mistakes cannot be covered with a brush stroke; they must be scraped off with steel wool down to the board itself. Even then, there is danger of marring the whiteness and smoothness of the board, so it is best just not to make mistakes.

Let us see just what this means. With every fine brush stroke, I must be aware of the final result, not at that moment evident. This blue that I am now putting on is only a part of an eventual violet. I have planned it that way. The later layers of red, or the later lines of blue of different intensity, will modify what I have just done, will further develop the real objective. Such planning is involved in every inch of the board. I must work with a small section at a time, for such technique does not gallop across a board.

At hand I have my sketches, my drawings, my notes—all my data for preplanning. Yet even these I modify as I go on my way, for my goal may keep changing as my project develops. Thus is drudgery transvalued by creativity.

I think that the reader will see in the care that must be taken, and in the preliminary planning, an analogy to the painting of murals. There, too, the quick sketches and the spontaneous small drawings must be combined with calculation and preplanning of the end-in-view. The techniques differ, but one fact is common to both a tempera painting and a mural: the painter cannot see his painting synthetically until it is completed.

Materials and Equipment

If you decide to explore the possibilities of tempera suggested in the previous chapter, what equipment will you need and how can it best be used?

Here is the "practical" portion of this book, the chapter to which you will most often refer. Therefore, I invite you to look over my shoulder, to see what materials I need, to find out how I use them—and then to modify what you have observed to your own requirements.

Naturally, I can offer you only the results of my own experience. With some experimentation of your own, you will doubtless develop other methods and other uses of material to fill in the tentative patterns here set forth. This is true of any medium. Who can dogmatically dictate the kind of brush or pigment or method of application? Who, in short, would dare to offer a foolproof road to achievement, an infallible recipe for good painting in any medium? If one could, then fools would be artists and good paintings a dime a dozen.

In the following detailed account, I merely deal more specifically with the means of attaining the values that I have previously discussed. The suggestions I offer may well be related to the plates which illustrate stages of tempera painting. When I offer trade names of materials, I merely suggest some that I have found to be satisfactory. You may find others more suited to your own purpose in the use of tempera. Consider the following to be only my own preferences.

THE SURFACE

For the surface of my tempera paintings I use $\frac{1}{8}''$ thickness of Tempered Masonite for paintings up to 36" in either direction. For larger paintings I use $\frac{3}{16}''$ thickness. For paintings of "mural size," say with a dimension of more than 56", where absolute rigidity is important, I use $\frac{3}{8}''$ or $\frac{1}{2}''$ Vehisote (a Homosote product).

Wood panels, also mounted or unmounted cottons or canvases, are quite good. With textile surfaces, no roughening is necessary, and four or five coats of the priming later described is sufficient, instead of the seven to ten coats used on boards.

I use the smooth side of the Masonite, filing it to the roughness I desire. I prefer not to use its already roughened surface, partly because the too mechanically even texture of its rough side asserts itself no matter how many coats of priming are used. Since both sides of Vehisote are of the same texture, this problem does not there arise.

To prepare the smooth surface of my board, I use a coarse steel file. My purpose is to adapt the board to a greater retention of the priming. I roughen the smooth surface, not too deeply, in all directions irregularly until the surface looks like a badly scratched windowpane.

Sizing the surface: Use a double boiler of one quart or more capacity. The lower part of the boiler will, of course, contain the water for heating. Into the upper section put, for the preparation of three or four boards of 30" x 36" size, the glue and gelatin. I use three standard size squares of glue of animal hide (preferably rabbit skin). A good glue is French Chardin Pantin glue, squares of which measure 6" x 7½" and weigh 3 ounces each; it is well to remember the weight in case you get glue already broken into small bits. With this I use two standard size squares of gelatin, 3½" x 8½", weight ¼ ounce each.

In the upper part of the boiler I put ¾ quart or more of water, enough to cover the broken up glue and gelatin completely, and then let it soak overnight. Then I heat it in double boiler until the glue dissolves completely. I stir the mixture occasionally as it is heating. It must not boil. The result is a "concentrated" glue solution. Any portion of it that you wish to prepare should be mixed in a pail or deep pan, say of two gallon capacity, with water, one portion of glue solution to fifteen parts of water; this is your glue solution to be used throughout.

Smear this blue sizing—solution—on both sides of your surface and on the edges, one coat.

Priming: While the glue is heating, mix zinc oxide and whiting in equal proportion (precipitated chalk or plaster of Paris). For about three boards one pound of each will do. Pour enough of your warm glue solution into your mixture to form, with stirring, a paste of the consistency of heavy honey. Add 2½ ounces of damar varnish (or mastic varnish, or a good grade of stand oil, or Navy specification spar varnish, or a half and half mixture of varnish and oil—your own experience and preferences will guide you later). You may increase or decrease the amount of varnish and oil, depending on whether you want a harder or softer ground—the more varnish you use, of course, the harder the ground will be. For a very hard ground, about 4¼ ounces of the varnish may be used.

As you add the varnish to the glue and zinc-chalk mixture, mix and agitate by constant stirring or with an egg beater for about an hour. This will be a hard job. The varnish must be so completely stirred that no trace of the singular little eyelets are visible when you finish stirring. Then, and only then, may you dilute this hardly flowing paste with more of the lukewarm glue solution. Add enough glue solution with stirring, to make a thin milklike mixture. The thinner the mixture, the better the "reflecting" surface will be—that is why I use thin coats of priming and so many of them. On this mechanical detail some of the best qualities of your painting will depend.

When your glue-sized board is dry, you are ready to apply seven to ten coats of priming—four to six coats with textile surfaces. Be sure that your priming solution is stirred frequently as you use it, to prevent settling of ingredients. Put priming coats on both sides and edges to prevent warping of the surface and peeling of the coatings. If the priming becomes thicker, dilute it with more of the lukewarm glue solution. Priming is applied with a 3" or 4" soft bristle brush, for a hard brush will leave ridges difficult to eliminate. Brush the first coat on in all directions and in irregular order. Each of the following coats goes on in a single direction, but in alternating order—e.g., the second coat may be applied from side to side, the third coat up and down, etc. All coats, excepting the last one, may be applied only when the preceding coat has dried completely. The last coat should be brushed on while the one preceding it is slightly damp. You may test this with a finger, but exert no pressure. Drying time between coats is usually one to three hours—you now see why I prepare all my boards for about a year at one time.

When your surface is thoroughly dry, sand with coarse, and then fine sandpaper to the degree of smoothness required for various effects. A coarser surface will ultimately give a powdery, dry tone to your painting.

For a semi-fine finish for the coarser kind of cross-hatching, I use Armour & Co. Flint-Bull's Head No. 64 or Imperial Flint Paper 2/0. If I intend an extremely fine final painting and therefore want a smoother, harder surface, I use the maximum amount of varnish or oil in the priming and give a third sanding with a fine steel wool, such as Imperial Steel Wool No. OO. To prevent scratching the surface, the wad of steel wool should be rubbed first against a piece of smooth hard wood, such as oak.

After the sanding, spray (or brush on) a 5% formaline solution. Be sure, first, to clean off the loose powder on the board.

Now the painting surface is ready. Your care up to this point will repay you amply, for you have prepared a surface that will not be *covered*, but which will reflect through all your subsequent painting. Its white, and its light, is already an integral part of your painting, even before you have decided what to paint.

PRELIMINARY SKETCHES

As I have previously indicated, you may be working on an already completed painting which you are translating into tempera. In that case, much of your preliminary work is done.

More and more, however, you will plan your tempera paintings from your initial encounter with the landscape or the subject. You will then prepare more or less detailed sketches and drawings in graphical media. You will make color notations or use some quick medium like water color or gouache or oil for a preliminary sketch or sketches. You will find such initial drawing and sketching in the illustrations accompanying this chapter. Note that with experience, such preliminary data will be fragmentary, less detailed, more sketchy, more in the nature of notes or memoranda. There might be much deviation in the final painting as compared to your earlier sketches.

At first, however, it is well to prepare detailed work before beginning the painting and then to follow such plans faithfully until control of tempera is well advanced. There is, of course, no rigid prescription. Methods vary. You must consider your preparatory work as memoranda, detailed enough for your memory and your needs. Remember that possibly your final tempera painting will be done in your studio some considerable time after your preliminary sketch work.

Your final step is to prepare a contour line drawing on tracing paper. This must be the exact size of the painting, for it will be transferred onto the board. On the reverse side of the tracing paper, smear, with a cotton pad, pulverized hard graphite (or charcoal). Blow a light spray of fixative on the graphite to keep it from soiling the board. Lay the tracing paper carefully on the board, graphite side on the board, and trace the drawing with a hard, blunt-pointed tool, such as a 9H pencil or the pointed handle of a brush. This will result in a sufficiently faint drawing that will not "bloom" through even a thin film of paint. In the illustration on page 30, you may see such a final drawing and examine its functional relation to the painting.

PAINTING

We must now consider the pigments necessary for your tempera painting and the types of emulsion you will use as their binder.

Emulsions: I like to prepare two kinds of emulsion for my colors, a casein emulsion for underpainting only and an egg varnish emulsion for all other layers of painting. However, either emulsion may be used throughout.

For the casein emulsion, use 1 ounce (by weight) of Casein Merck (according to Hammarsten) or any other pure casein. Stir well into 7 ounces of distilled water. Let the solution stand for three or four hours, then add 1 teaspoonful of 5% ammonia solution (if ammonia solution is difficult to obtain, use two small cubes of ammonia carbonate dissolved in a teaspoonful of water, crushing the cubes in the water to facilitate the dissolving). Stir continuously as you add the ammonia. Into this stir $\frac{1}{5}$ teaspoon of sodium orthophenyl phenate. Heat very slowly, well below the boiling point, until the ammonia odor evaporates and the liquid is clear, transparent, and of the consistency of honey. One ounce of this casein solution is then diluted with 6 to 8 ounces of distilled water.

This casein emulsion may be bought in prepared form to save time and trouble. I always prefer "homemade" products where they are possible, and I believe students should be familiar with their materials from the bottom up. However, you will find Shiva prepared casein emulsion (Shiva is a Chicago firm) quite satisfactory. This is of thick consistency and should be diluted to desired thinness with distilled water.

Whether you use a prepared casein emulsion or make your own, you now have a binder for underpainting — or complete painting — your tempera. You may add $\frac{1}{2}$ fluid ounce of damar to this emulsion, while it is undiluted, for greater binding power, constantly stirring until the mixture is even in texture. When you use your emulsion in painting, add distilled water if it is necessary, to maintain the thinness and "brushable" consistency.

For all painting after the underpainting, you may use an egg varnish emulsion; this, at least, is my preference. To prepare this, break and stir one whole egg. Then add damar varnish or a good grade of stand oil, about $\frac{1}{4}$ to $\frac{1}{3}$ the bulk of the egg. Add 5 drops of oil of cloves. Add these ingredients in this order, stirring vigorously at each stage; otherwise they will not mix. Add to your mixture twice to three times the amount of distilled water, stirring thoroughly. Strain through loosely woven cheesecloth to catch unbroken particles of egg.

I do not want to be too dogmatic about the use of casein emulsion as the binder for underpainting and the egg tempera for all other painting. You may want to use one or the other throughout your painting. All sorts of variations on this main theme are possible; you must consider these instructions as a skeletal outline only.

Colors: The color range of the pigments I use both for underpainting and later painting will be found in the summary of materials at the end of this chapter. Be sure that your dry pigments are well ground into a fine powder. I find, for dry pigments, that Permanent Pigments of Cincinnati are dependably prepared. Most of them are lime-proof. Those that I find too coarse for my liking I regrind in a china mortar with an ordinary hard ceramic pestle. I have also used, with good effect, earth colors from various parts of the country: Tennessee, Virginia, Michigan, etc. These must be well washed and ground.

Mix each powdered pigment with distilled water to a jellylike consistency in a cup or glass jar of 2 or 3 ounce capacity. Add to the mixture a small amount—10 or 15 drops for 3 ounces of the pigment solution—of the egg-damar-oil of cloves emulsion just described.

If you keep your colors in cups or jars topped with distilled water to prevent drying, there is no reason why they should not last five to six months. Some of my colors are older than that and still retain good texture and brilliancy. It is well to change the top distilled water every two or three months to help keep the colors clear and clean.

Palette and Brushes: An excellent palette—although you will doubtless devise your own—is a lightweight structure similar to a tea table with a shelf half way between top and bottom. It is about 24" high and is movable on casters. It has a plate glass top, the reverse side of which is enameled white. This top is countersunk 1", or may be bordered by a 1" high ledge. The container for the colors is a U-shaped one-sided tin channel, the vertical depth of which is 1" (the height of the ledge) and the horizontal depth of which is about 1½". This channel has sections at 1" intervals into which are placed "scoops" of paint sufficient to last two or three days (see drawing on page 24). Now, when the paint is not being used, put a large, flat, wet sponge in the middle of the palette and cover the whole thing with a piece of glass resting on the ledges. This keeps the paint moist and nearly air-proofs the inside space.

Brushes for your underpainting: Here you can use, for the most part, a ¾" to 1" flat sable brush, for the smooth and even tonal underpainting. Where you seek uneven underpainting, especially for large areas, you will find useful a 1" to 1½" finer quality bristle brush. For the rest of your painting, which involves the coarse to fine cross-hatched lines, you will want flat sable brushes from ⅛" to 1" and No. 1 to 10 round sables. These brushes will run the whole range from coarse to finest "graphical" usage. Oil brushes of the fine short bristle variety come in handy for use with emulsion that is strong in adhesive power (more varnish). Such emulsion is used in large areas with cross-hatching that is in one color and one tone and coarsely applied.

Underpainting: Now that we have the board prepared, our colors and emulsions ready, and our materials at hand, we are ready for the first stages of the underpainting. Here I prefer to use the casein emulsion.

Whether you are working on the underpainting or the later stages, it is important to note how to use your emulsion. You dip your brush into the emulsion, absorbing as much of it as possible and wiping off the excess on the lip of the container. Then you take up the paint, as you need it, in the emulsion-saturated brush, renewing the emulsion as it is used up. To avoid contamination of colors as you use the same brush for different colors, wipe the brush on a moist rag that you keep on the palette. If you want your brush strokes to consist of fine—or coarser—lines at any phase of your painting, press the root of the bristles of your paint-filled brush onto the palette till the bristles spread like a fan and touch the surface

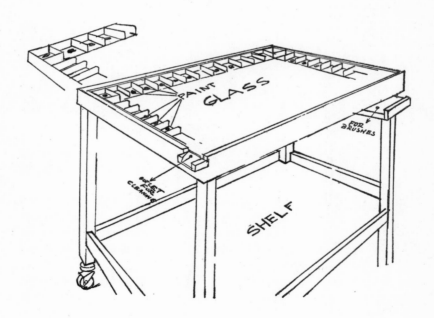

lightly. Repeat this frequently since the bristles will merge eventually. Above all do not go over the same brush stroke too many times. Where a solid, dense stroke is needed, the above operation is not necessary. It will take a lot of practice to get this kind of handling of your brush under full control.

It is always an important procedure to start your painting with a thin, even coat of underpainting, leaving out those areas which are to remain white in the completed painting. In the underpainting, your problem is to develop the basic tones and designs of the picture, to use colors that not only give the dominant colors of finished objects, but that also lay the foundation for patterns and spatial relations. No dogmatic rule can be set forth; your problem here is obviously one of composition and creative intent as well as of technique of painting. In a naturalistic painting your underpainting may bring out the dominant colors and patterns of specific objects, in abstract painting you may underpaint thinly with dark and light areas and tones that emphasize over-all design and spatial patterns. Or you may combine various modes and purposes.

All that I can say is that in your underpainting you are laying the foundation, presenting and accenting the theme which all your later painting will elaborate. It is an important stage toward your final result.

As I have already indicated, you should use a ¾" to 1" brush for the thin, "solid" painting that your underpainting usually calls for. You will, of course, use different brushes when your method differs—e.g., a larger brush of coarser bristles for uneven painting in large areas.

You will find an example of this stage of a painting in the illustrations on pages 32 and 33. It will be instructive to compare the earlier stages to the final painting.

Later Painting: Now we come to the stage of the painting for which no prescription can be given; only a few suggestions can be offered, and the rest is up to you.

Since you will now be working, for the most part, with fine lines, I suggest, but not dogmatically, the egg emulsion as it is somewhat more transparent and better adapted to the kind of technique I am discussing. You will then use your finer brushes—your ⅛" to 1" sable flat brushes and your No. 1 to 10 round sables.

As you use the cross-hatching of lines, the number of layers you apply will depend upon your purpose—the complexity of color and tonal relations in a particular area, the depth and range of undertones and overtones, the density of color called for, etc.

No formula can be given, for you are now pretty much upon your creative own. You may note, however, that in general the deeper under layers should carry the dominant tones and colors of the final objects or designs, for the under layers are the first carriers of the light that is reflected from the basic white background.

Earlier layers of cross-hatching should be coarser than later ones. These first layers have the function of bringing your objects and designs in any part of the picture into plastic visibility. With the first layer or layers comes the contours, thicknesses, shapes, shadows and spatial depths—it is your concept coming into realization. Examine the illustration of the first stage after the underpainting and compare it to the underpainting stage and the final stage to see what values emerge (pages 32 and 33).

Perhaps you will use, in some areas of your painting, five or six more layers of finer and finer cross-hatched lines, but all are refinements of this earlier critical stage in which your basic idea first takes a really specific shape.

Remember, for it cannot be too often said, that you are using pure colors, without white. The blending that with oil or water color is accomplished on the palette can come only visually with tempera, through your successive layers. The only white is that of the board. You will let that white through in varying degrees by the wideness or denseness of your cross-hatching and the thinness or thickness of your color application. You may want to experiment with some color mixing on the palette, but be careful to maintain the transparency of your medium by means of thinness of the mixture, or your earlier layers, as well as the white of the board, will be lost.

Another important point: you may, with later layers, intensify or deepen the preceding colors of objects or designs, but you can never again lighten them, for the light is already under the preceding layers. To attempt to add light by the use of white would only make an opaque spot and hide the values you have worked so hard to achieve. Your mistakes can only be corrected by scraping with steel wool or penknife and starting that area over again.

Let us take an obvious example, without subtle complications. Suppose you want to achieve a purplish blue. You may start with red and overpaint with a blue, or you may reverse this order. Your choice of first color will depend upon which tone you want to dominate the final color. It is the lower layer that will probably be stronger, although much depends upon your technique in that particular area.

Sometimes you will want your cross-hatched lines to be visible in the final painting. At other times you may want to tone them down or obliterate them after they have accomplished their function of color-blending. The illustrations in this book will show such varied treatments. To soften or hide cross-hatched lines, add a final layer to that part of the picture where that effect is desired. This layer will be a thin, solid, even, transparent film of the local color of the object in a naturalistic work, or the color of the relational tone in an abstract work.

I have previously indicated that in addition to the blending of colors from the board outward through the successive layers, there is also two-dimensional blending. You may place lines of color close together to produce the blending. This is especially useful for certain purposes. Where you want to indicate a strong direction of light or of movement, you may blend colors in that direction without cross-hatching, but rather by close, fine parallel lines of colors which are elements in the blend that you seek.

For example, the purple that I have spoken of, secured through layers of red and blue, may also be obtained through fine lines of blue and red laid side by side. This technique may, perhaps, indicate the oblique direction of the rays of the sun or even its intensity of light, or it may give motion in the direction in which a horse is running. However, we are now entering matters that do not lend themselves to description by words. These are intangibles acquired by observing the work of others and experimenting for yourself.

POLISHING

The purpose of polishing your completed painting is to preserve the tempera. This is more necessary with finely sanded boards, since they are smoother and less absorbent than cottons and canvases. Nevertheless, I prefer boards as better carriers of the smoothness and light which are so fundamental in tempera.

Let your completed painting dry for about two weeks. It is then ready for a "base" varnish. Mix 3 parts of damar varnish or a good grade of mastic varnish with 1 part of spirits of turpentine. If this is too thick, thin it further with spirits of turpentine. Apply it to your painting with a wide camel hair or sable brush, say 2″. The wider the brush the better.

After two to three weeks, when the painting is thoroughly dry, you may apply the final polish. Dissolve 1 disk (1½ ounces by weight), or more if you need it, of white beeswax (it is only the proportions that are important here) in a water bath, not directly over the flame. To your liquid wax add oil of turpentine, three times the amount of the wax (three of turpentine to one of liquid wax, by volume). Brush the warmed-up mixture onto the painting, wiping off any excess with a lintless rag. Let the painting dry for two or three days, then rub with hard pressed felt. To secure more sheen in the polish, you may add to the wax-turpentine mixture ½ ounce of damar or mastic varnish. If the varnish is increased to 1½ ounces, you may eliminate the base varnish (damar or mastic with spirits of turpentine) and get enough protection through the one coat, again brushed on warm with excesses wiped off. Since you will brush the polish on one area at a time, it is important that it be evenly applied. Especially be careful that there are no variations of thickness or ridges where areas overlap.

If there is too much sheen to the polish, which is more likely to be the case if you have used only the polishing coat with the larger quantity of varnish, you may dull it with a steel wool of the finest grade—e.g. Imperial Steel Wool OO. Be careful to do this with the least possible pressure, for obvious reasons.

Pen and ink studies. My
notebook contains many
of these for possible later
use as bases for tempera
painting.

29

The final transfer sketch above shows to what uses my notebook studies on the preceding page were put. Notice the smudge marks of the graphite on the other side of the tracing paper upon which this drawing was made.

This is the final product. Even here you will see liberties taken with the transfer sketch as the painting progressed.

THEIR DAY ALMOST OVER

MARINE STILL LIFE. *Above: Sketch after transfer to board. Below: Underpainting*

Further development of the same subject and, below, the final painting.

Notebook material for the painting
IN THE DAY'S WORK
(Complete painting on opposite page)

The pen and ink sketch opposite is an incidental "note," one figure
of which was used in the painting *SUNBATH*. The illustration at
the bottom of the opposite page is another example of a final transfer
sketch. Above is the completed painting.

Pencil sketch for a detail of the "Great Lakes Fisherman" mural, another detail of which is shown opposite.

Detail from the author's mural, painted in casein tempera for the
Lincoln Park, Michigan, Post Office.

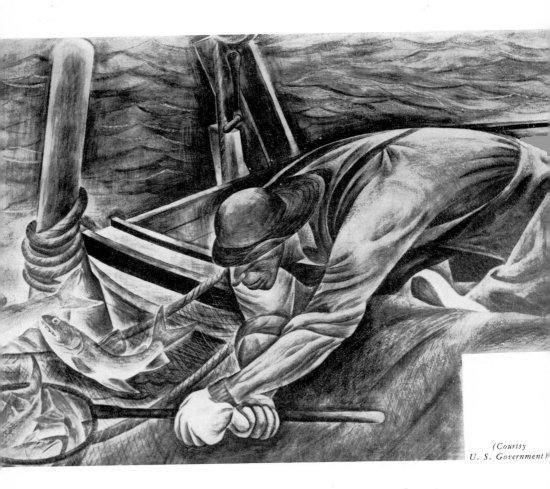

(Courtsy
U. S. Government)

39

DETAIL STUDY IN TEMPERA

SUMMARY OF MATERIALS

You may now find useful a list of the materials employed in the tempera painting I have described. Specific trade names and quantities depend upon circumstances and may be found by referring to the preceding text.

SURFACE

Board or Canvas

File

Glue (Animal Hide)

Gelatin

Double Boiler

Whiting (Precipitated Chalk)

Oxide of Zinc (Powdered)

Damar or Mastic Varnish or Stand Oil

Egg Beater

Brushes (3″ and 4″)

Sandpaper—Various Grades

Steel Wool OO

5% Formaline Solution

Two gallon Pail

PAINTING

Shiva Casein Emulsion—or

"Homemade" Casein Emulsion:
Casein
Distilled Water
5% Ammonia Solution or
Ammonia Carbonate
Sodium Orthophenyl Phenate

Damar or Mastic Varnish or Stand Oil

Egg

Oil of Cloves

Cheesecloth

Mortar and Pestle

Cups or Jars

Palette

Brushes
¾″ to 1″ Flat Sable
1″ to 1½″ Finer Bristle
⅛″ to 1″ Flat Sables
No. 1 to 10 Round Sables

Colors—Powdered Dry Pigments—
Those in italics not indispensable:
Cadmium Yellow Light (popularly known as Primrose)
Cadmium Yellow Dark
Cadmium Orange
Cadmium Red Light
Cadmium Red Deep
Mars Indian Red (Red Iron Oxide)
Venetian Red (Red Ochre)
Alizarin Rose Madder

SUMMARY OF MATERIALS (Continued)

Mars Violet (Violet Iron Oxide)	Chromium Hydroxide
Golden Oxide	*Chromium Oxide (Opaque)*
Yellow Ochre	*Phthalocyanine Green*
Raw Sienna	Cerulean Blue
Raw Umber	Cobalt Blue
Burnt Umber	Ultramarine Blue
Van Dyke Brown	*Phthalocyanine Blue*
Terre Verde (Green)	*Prussian Blue*
Viridian Deep	Ivory Black

POLISHING

2″ or 3″ Sable Brush	Beeswax
Damar or Mastic Varnish	Steel Wool OO
Spirits of Turpentine	Felt Pad

Tempera—When and Where

From the preceding chapters, the reader has already noted some limitations in the use of tempera, if one wishes to exploit its most distinctive qualities. These limitations pertain to time and place.

Let me hasten to modify this first statement. By "limitations" I definitely do not mean "handicaps." The conditions under which tempera paintings can be produced are opportunities rather than impediments, just as are the conditions imposed upon, let us say, fresco painting. I merely indicate here once again that *my* use of tempera demands different conditions from those of oil or other media.

First, and most obviously, tempera is not an on-the-spot medium. I have indicated that the landscape or portrait on which you want to work must first be studied in other media, in drawings and sketches, more or less complete and detailed. They are your preliminaries for the days upon days that await you in the studio.

The time element further imposes upon you the condition that you can do only a few tempera paintings each year. I myself consider this to be a wholesome fact. Since your ideas will likely far outstrip the possibility of using this medium exclusively, you will avoid the deadening habit of working with only one type of medium.

This leads me to a question that I have been asked more than once: "If tempera were a quicker medium, if there were not this time limitation, would you use this medium and this technique for everything you paint?"

I can honestly answer "No." Still, it is difficult for me to say why I do choose tempera for certain of my works: what qualities in an already completed water color or oil or gouache lead me to translate that painting into tempera, or what aspects of a landscape or still life seem to demand this more ambitious treatment. Such judgments are matters of personal taste for each painter to decide.

In my own case, the only case I can discuss, I know that there are certain scenes that call for coarse brush strokes or daubs with a palette knife or a thumb. Then there are moods that demand the fragility of pastel or the delicacy—and strength—of water color. Every painter will know what I mean.

I advise the beginner to do detailed preliminary work at first. With experience, this first work can be shortened. In my first early experiments,

I repainted from completed gouaches, not because the originals dissatisfied me but because I perceived qualities which I could emphasize and enhance by this "new" method. Now, nearly always, as I have said, my decisions are prefigured. I am outdoors, ready to paint in a "quick" medium. I study the scene. My original plans go up in smoke. "This," I say, "cries for tempera." Instead of a finished painting, my on-the-spot product is a series of fragmentary drawings and color sketches, feverishly gathered, and very sketchy indeed. These graphic memoranda I file away for the future time that I can give to the painting I intend. Now my temperas are nearly all premeditated from the very start, my preliminary work relative to the final result.

All this I have said in a previous context. I repeat it here to emphasize the time and care that not only the painting, but also the planning of tempera should take.

I have been asked, "How can you endure the long hours spent on the innumerable cross-hatched lines of a tempera painting? Doesn't the tedium destroy the creative enthusiasm that originally motivated your work?"

Do long hours destroy the sculptor's first enthusiasm? Or the mural painter's? Or any craftsman's? Is there not always a joy in his work for any kind of worker who sees what he is doing from beginning to end?

For me, there is no tedious moment in this tempera painting. With each step of the process, the painter sees values emerge and unfold; he learns, with experience, even to change those intended values as he paints. He is like the traveler who knows his objective, but who, with each fresh step, may find new ways of reaching it.

In every act of creation, there is the joyful moment of creation, the long term of gestation, the pain of parturition. So in art, whether the process from beginning to end be long or short. Always the tedium and the labor are lightened and vivified by the impetus of the first spontaneous act of creation and the vision of what the end, the goal, will be.

One further value that I find in tempera, which fits into this chapter, is that translucent tempera is well adapted to our own cultural milieu. It is adapted to new architectural trends, not fads of the moment, but enduring trends. This milieu is free from unnecessary and cumbersome "decoration," plastic protrusions, thick and heavy appendages. It is free from capricious, undulating surfaces. It is in key with the even smoothness of the tempera picture surface. It is free from darkness and murkiness, in harmony with the translucence of tempera color and tonality. It absorbs to its decorative demands the smooth flow of tempera—even utilizing such "practical" qualities as the possibility of doing away with weighty framing, or any framing at all.

Again, I want to avoid the suggestion of "selling" tempera to the exclusion of other media. Tempera has its function—its important time and place—and it is that function to which this book points.

Tempera—For Whom?

Having considered such "practical" matters as pigments and brushes and glue and double boilers, also the "whys and whens" of tempera painting, let us discuss a more personal problem.

For whom is tempera painting adapted? How advanced must a student be to consider tempera as a medium? Is there any reason for an accomplished artist, who is already having great pleasure in—and good returns from—his work in another medium, to dabble with or to go seriously into the tempera technique I have described?

I shall begin with the beginner. The fact that my use of tempera is a "sophisticated" technique need not frighten the early student. He may develop stage fright from my previous remarks about preliminary sketches and complicated techniques. Yet my own teaching experience has proved that students may use this tempera method early in their studies. Those who have developed even elementary ability with any other medium—preferably water color—may start experimenting with tempera coincidentally with oil and other media. The well-rounded painter must have many techniques at his command, many keys to the varied doors he seeks to open, and tempera painting has rewards different from those won by other modes of expression.

Here is a warning. The road to which I point is a hard and tortuous one. Many good works in water color, or even oil, may be matters of minutes, or hours, or days. When you begin a tempera painting, you must be prepared to work on it for weeks. You must be prepared for days of planning, for numberless fine brush strokes, for patient attention to detail, for eye burning and seat callousing hour upon hour.

Is there anything about such rigors to attract the advanced student or the painter who is successful with another medium?

I think so. To use tempera is certainly not a confession of, an escape from, failure with another medium. For me, tempera became, a number of years ago, the joy of exploration, the discovery of a new way of enhancing and enriching the occasional "classic" of another medium.

After all, the artist who turns to tempera does not abandon other media or methods. I should not presume to advise my fellow painters and students. I merely hope that they will be led, not by this account but by their own investigations, to evaluate the possibilities of tempera. I believe that tempera will have a growing appeal for accomplished men and women who constantly seek new means to age-old ends.

Let's talk business. If your dealer—and honestly, you *students* among the readers will some day have dealers—sets a price on your work, he evaluates it, for the most part, in terms of its size and the recalcitrance of the medium. An oil painting will sell for more than a water color, because there is a public belief that oil painting is more difficult and takes longer. For some reason seven hundred square inches, too, are worth more proportionally than two hundred square inches. Your dealer is not trying to reduce art to arithmetic. He does not believe that oil is "better" than water color, nor that a large picture is intrinsically "better" than a small one. He merely knows his buyers.

Unfortunately, no such quantitative evaluation has as yet been put on the tempera technique. The public that has learned to judge by size and medium (among the works of the same artist) has still no conception of the difficulties this new use of medium involves. Even some critics are unaware of how the values of this tempera technique are attained. Until there is more general understanding that hours of oil or gouache equal weeks of tempera, the road to which I point is a road of sacrifice. Either you must have time to spend on tempera or you must be willing to use time that might be more lucratively employed.

So there you have it. Who shall paint in tempera? "Everyone," is the judgment of the artist within me. Yet my conscience leads me to the "practical" warnings above. But who knows? Perhaps the road of artistic inclination is the eventual way to "good business."

Subject Matter

The preceding chapters have been essentially concerned with the materials and technique of tempera painting. I would not dare to be pontifical, or even to offer suggestions, about the painter's choice of subject or the goals he ought to seek. For here the artist brings his own modes of perception, his entire past experience, to bear upon the materials with which he has chosen to work.

There are esthetic philosophers who, like Benedetto Croce, insist that art is entirely spiritual, wholly a matter of the imagination, and that the physical work of the artist is a sort of appendage outside the true realm of art.

Why is it that such contempt for technique is always expressed by those who have no technique? Why is the artist himself never afraid to dirty his hands with the "ordinary" materials about him? Why is the artist able to plod along unromantically with his paint or his clay or his textiles or his blueprints? I think it is because the artist knows that, in art, means and ends, content and form, are inseparable; because the artist's vision is no vaporous figment in an ivory tower, but is rather a conception of the possibilities inherent in the materials of everyday life.

Estheticism that expresses contempt for the materials of art is merely an escape from art itself. If history teaches anything about art, it is that art arises out of the narrow and difficult experiences of ordinary life, that art is man's attempt to enrich and broaden those activities, and that its subject matter is everywhere.

For those who seek a moral, then, I have only this moral to offer: that there is no one right way to paint, no one right subject matter for art. Art is as varied as the needs and pursuits of men. Its only dogma is that it has no dogmas.

All that a painter can do is to work with integrity and sincerity. To his work he brings the heightened perceptions that have made him choose art as a career. If he is intelligent, his product will be socially intelligible. He must not be afraid to experiment, to try new materials, new techniques, new goals.

Painting, like all art, has its social functions—to transform the burdensome routines of existence into the more joyful activities of life. What art has accomplished and is accomplishing reaches only into a few corners of that existence. In those corners, art is the signpost to the values that we may some day find in all experience.

Sketches and notes by the author.

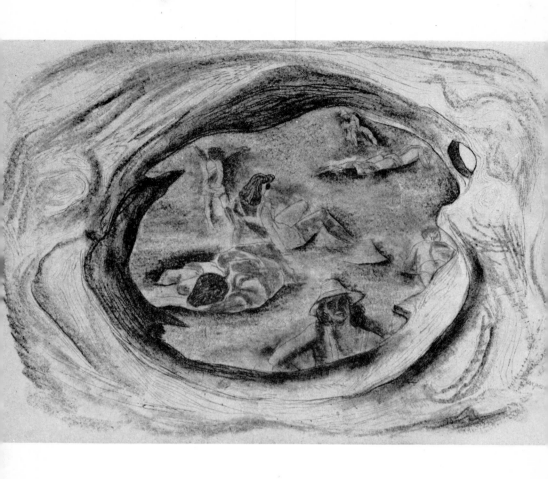

The pencil sketch above compared to the final tempera opposite shows how much rearrangement and deviation is possible between the spontaneous first sketch and the carefully planned product.

DRIFTWOOD. *The completed painting by the author.*

Preliminary sketches, three of which were used in the painting opposite.

SUNTAN. *The completed painting by the author.*

END OF THE DAY

POD GATHERER

SLEEPING EARTH

AFTERNOON SKIING

(Courtesy Hall Collection, University of Nebraska)

DEPARTING BOAT

CAR FERRY

JANUARY

ALONG THE TURNPIKE

NEW ENGLAND SIESTA

NOON AT A COUNTRY FAIR

THINGS WE CHILDREN LIKE

PIGEON

REMNANTS OF SUMMER

SANDSCAPE

SATURDAY AFTERNOON

MORNING

WILD FLOWERS

THE ARTIST AND HIS WIFE

SUNDAY AFTERNOON

LUNCH'N MUSIC

CONTRIBUTING ARTISTS

The remaining pages represent a selection of tempera paintings by leading American artists which give the student the opportunity of studying and analyzing the different styles that characterize the work of each painter.

CHARLES SHEELER   "Mechanization"

(Opposite) THOMAS HART BENTON   Final Section of Missouri Mural

REGINALD MARSH   "Adults Ten Cents, Children Five"

PETER HURD   "The Made Tank"

BEN SHAHN   "World's Greatest Comics"

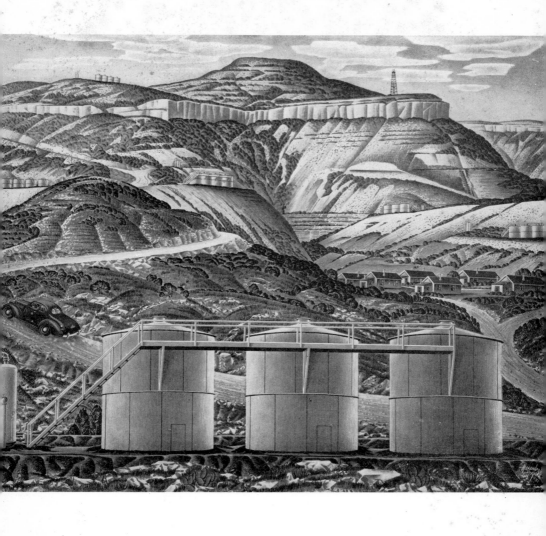

ALEXANDRE HOGUE   "Pecos Escarpment"